Introduction

To be quite honest, I had no plans to write a second book on this subject but I have been encouraged to do so by a few reviewers who enjoyed the first 'ONLY IN CYPRUS' but felt it was too short, so thus the second one. Less pictures more words.

I have had a pleasing success with ONLY IN CYPRUS and have received some very nice positive reviews, but there were a few not so positive. One reviewer called it 'NONSENSE' and another said it was 'EXAGERATED' for the sake of humour. With hand on heart I say that although it was written very much 'tongue in cheek', all the stories are absolutely true as are the ones in this book.

So, as before, pour yourself a nice large long Ouzo, put your feet up and laugh out loud to this equally funny, (and true), insight into Cyprus life.

Yiayia (Grandma)

We have all got or had one. In my case it's 'had', may she rest in peace. I only ever knew one of my Yiayias, mums side.

My yiayias passport photo.

Yiayia played a huge role in my life as a child growing up in the UK, she was very important. Well all Yiayias are important but in Cyprus they are almost indispensable.

Mum and Dad go to work to earn the money for the repayments for the two Mercedes, the house and to put Halloumi on the table, but Yiayia does EVERYTHING else! She will spend all day dusting, sweeping and mopping the house from the rafters to the cellar and then do the outside! All the while she is doing this she will be mumbling under her breath how disgustingly filthy her Daughter in law is. In between this marathon task she will also prepare a veritable banquet for everyone for when they get in AND look after the kids! Yiayia, with that cute, soft and cuddly exterior, can also be tough and sometimes even wicked! Wicked? How so? I'll tell you how by relating a TRUE story that actually happened to me and I lived to tell the tale.

Now picture this; A cold Winters evening, a roaring fire, (we had them in those days), myself and my three younger siblings sat in front of it on a rug after being bathed squeaky clean and being read to by Yiayia...Aww! You might be forgiven for thinking that we were being read 'Little Red Riding Hood' or 'Jack and the Beanstalk' but you couldn't be further from the truth because Yiayia never read us such 'SKATA' (shit) no! She was reading to us from the Bible!! You might say 'what's wrong with that?' well there is nothing wrong with that...occasionally, but for a 3, 5, 7, and 9 year old I think nursery rhymes would have been better...

Anyway, this one act doesn't make her wicked but what follows does. As I said, the four of us sat in front of the fire not listening to a word Yiayia was saying, it was all Greek to us anyway, and getting very bored, well I know I was, I picked up the tin, (it came in a tin then), of 'Johnsons Baby Powder' and decided to throw it at my sister Mary....what? The tin hit Mary on the knee and being a drama queen she screamed the house down! She was running around the room flaying her arms around like ET! I thought it was funny, her screaming I mean. Yiayia slammed the huge Bible closed and slowly got up from her chair towering above us like a Black Ninja skyscraper, (she was over 6ft tall). She quickly transformed into something that was a far cry from the nurturing, caring and God fearing Yiayia that had been reading 'The Good Samaritan' to us seconds earlier, she turned into 'GODZILLZA' hurling some hideously unsavory and very unholy words and phrases, all directed at me! It started gently with 'BELO BLUSMA' (mad person), and 'GAOURI' (Donkey), and progressed rapidly to 'GAMO TO GERATO SOU' (Fuck your horn)....to this day I am yet to work out what that means exactly? Perhaps she was referring to my 'Devils horn'? Anyway, needless to say she was angry! She grabbed both of my wrists with one hand, (she could do that), and with the other slapped me hard on the back of the head. "If you do that again I will burn your hand with that poker!" she said, in Greek as she couldn't speak English yet.

After comforting Mary and reassuring my other sister Doula and brother Dino that Mary was going to live, she sat back in her chair and opened her Bible. As she read I remember drifting off and thinking to myself, 'She wouldn't actually burn me...would she?' There was only one sure way of finding out anything was better than hearing how many people walked past the man laying by the side of the road... again!

Mary sat opposite me and was still sniffing and sniveling. I felt my fingers slowly tip toeing towards the baby powder tin and yes, once more, I threw it at my sister! This time unfortunately, I threw it a bit harder, also a bit higher and it hit poor Mary on the crease of her eyebrow! Blood started to spurt out everywhere! I froze in pure panic! Yiayia was up like a shot....now this next bit is what makes me believe only a wicked person would act in such a way. BEFORE rushing to Mary's aid, who was now bleeding to death, Yiayia took the time to pick up the poker and shove it into the flames and then said to me, 'TORA NA THIS TI THA SOU GAMO!' (Wait and see what I'm going to do to you). Only then did she wrap my sister's head in a tea towel! So is that not premeditated?

She drew out from the fire the Red glowing poker and grabbed both my hands by the wrists and asked me which hand had thrown the tin? I dutifully told her and she did nothing more but stab it with the hot poker filling the air with the stench of burning human flesh! She then tied me to the Newel post of the staircase with her huge apron strings and there I stayed until mum got home. YEP!! I'll let you decide who the wicked one was, me or Yiayia. ☺

So when you are in Cyprus and you see all those cute Black clad old ladies walking around as if butter wouldn't melt in their mouth.....DON'T BE FOOLED!!

^===^===^

Fayito (Food)

Food is a subject that is very high up on the priority list in the Cypriot household, to the point of distraction. If you are blessed with a dinner invite in Cyprus, do NOT eat that day! Seriously! Even the poorest household will put enough food on the table that would easily solve the Worlds hunger problem, (Especially if Yiayia has prepared it). There is a Cypriot phrase, and I apologize profusely for writing it here, but it's absolutely necessary and relevant to this subject. You would speak this phrase when relaying to a third party about how much food you had to eat. The saying goes; 'EMBIXAN MAS GE BOU TON GOLO' (They even poked it up our arse)....sorry! There is no way you would leave a Cypriot table and be hungry.

The onslaught starts from the minute you have been greeted and seated. Typically, in an English household, you would probably see on the occasional tables some 'nibbles', i.e. Peanuts, Crisps and if you are really lucky, Cashew nuts. These serve the purpose of keeping you occupied until dinner is served.

In a Cypriot household you are already seated at the dining table because this is where all the socializing is done, and below is what you would expect to see on it.

I kid you not!

As you sit there staring at the, what you would think of as a banquet and not 'nibbles', you are faced with shouts from your hosts of 'FAE FAE' (Eat eat), and if you don't your hosts would be very offended. They will also apologize for having so little on the table, but it's deliberate so as not to spoil your appetite for the REAL food which is to follow! I don't know about you but that lot would keep me going for a week!

As you all sit around the table drinking copious amounts of Wine, Beer and your hosts homemade Tzivania, and perhaps getting Greek lessons, you realize that all the so called nibbles are gone and that's when the avalanche of food that is dinner is lovingly served. Dishes upon dishes of food that would feed the whole village! A baking tray of 'MAGARONIA TOU FOURNOU' a sort of Lasagna but replace the Lasagna strips with thick cut macaroni with a herby mince topped with a Béchamel sauce. Just one Cypriot portion of that and you are full. There is 'BOURGOURI' (Like Couscous), there is a huge Cypriot salad for each end of the table, 'TAVA' (Lamb and potato stew), there is a dish of 'GOUNELLI STIFADO' (Rabbit cooked in onions), there is 'GOTOBOULO ROSTO' (Roast Chicken) and not to forget the large tray of Lemon roasted potatoes!

The table is brimming with every food imaginable and some! You gaze in awe at the task that confronts you and thank the powers that be that you are not alone, and anyway, it's not like there is a time limit. You are ordered to serve yourself and God help you if your plate is not full to capacity, you will hear things like, 'TROI SUN TON STROUFO' (He eats like a Sparrow), or 'THEN SOU ARESE?' (Don't you like it?).

The English eat in 20mins. Get up, wash up, and get on with their lives. The Cypriot meal time is an event to be savored and can take hours. So you have been eating and drinking for what seems like an eternity and you can't loosen your belt any more for fear of losing your trousers, just then your host announces in a proud voice...

'TA SOUVLAKIA INE SKETHO ETIMA' (The kebabs are nearly ready).

Yes, Bappou, (Granddad), has been outside lovingly tending the BBQ and the Pork kebabs are nearly ready....just in case!

NOW EAT!!

The Cypriot woman's every waking thought is, 'TI THA MAYIREPSO BOPSE?', (What shall I cook tonight?). My wife works in an office environment and she tells me the main topic of conversation every day is 'What are YOU cooking tonight?' In the Supermarket, you see them blocking the aisles whilst having a chat and you wait patiently to get past and what is the intriguing conversation they are engaged in? 'What are YOU cooking tonight?' At the store counter waiting to pay for your goods and the girl behind the counter is on her mobile phone, you listen in on her conversation while you tap the counter with irritation, what is she talking about? 'What are you cooking tonight?'. In the queue at the pharmacy waiting to collect your medication, the two women in front of you are in deep thought, suddenly one pipes up, 'THA GANO FASOLIA!' (I will do beans!). Women all over this island that is Cyprus have forgotten all their woes because this is the biggest woe of all....'What to cook tonight?'

^===^===^

To aftoginito (The Car.)

I touched on this subject in book one, but there is more, so much more. I hope you will forgive me if it sounds like I am tarring all Cypriots with the same brush but I am writing from my own personal experiences and can only convey what I have witnessed with my own eyes and ears….and I'm a Cypriot!

There are many different categories of vehicles that the Cypriot driver slots into. I will describe a few here for our entertainment.

'The Double Cab Pick Up Truck'

This is a very popular vehicle because of its multi-functional uses. The driver of this vehicle fancies himself as a bit of a 'rough shod outdoor type'. He likes to go hunting so he has a tailor made metal cage made that fits neatly in the back of the pickup. This is to put his hunting companions in....his dogs! This cage is removable so when he goes to the beach he has room for all the paraphernalia that goes with him, BBQ, Table and chairs etc. (see book One). It also serves as a removal van for transporting friends and families furniture to the tip... (the side of the road!). There is also plenty of room for his paint pots, tools, bags of cement for when he is in his 'I can fix anything' guise. Last but not least, it is a family car. Once in the Double cab bit, you can be forgiven for thinking you are in a luxury limousine, in fact, this IS what they are but with an extra bit stuck on the end for all the above uses. The added bonus for driving one of these is that you can park wherever you choose because of the 'my car is bigger than yours' syndrome!

'The Mercedes driver'

The Mercedes driver wouldn't be seen dead in a pickup truck, (unless it's a Mercedes). Although the Mercedes driver is driving a Mercedes it's the Bank that actually owns it. This man will get himself into debt just so he can say he drives a Mercedes, a status symbol, even though he has no status!! i.e. he is unemployed, has no savings and has blagged his way at the Bank and got a loan, probably with Dad as a guarantor. (obviously this doesn't apply to ALL Merc owners, but I know at least one). ☺ This driver can also park wherever he wants to because…..well because 'I have a Mercedes and that gives me the right' ….syndrome!

So we have established that he can't really afford his Mercedes but this doesn't stop him/her walking around with their nose in the air with a 'I am mightier than thou' attitude. Unfortunately with all the acting skills in the World, this sham is seen through by the less fortunate over and over. Here are a couple of examples of what I mean.

One day I drove into my local petrol station and parked my Mazda Demio by a pump. A Mercedes driver pulled up at the pump next to mine. In Cyprus we still get 'Pump service', that is, a nice man comes to your car and you wind your window down and tell him your needs. It won't surprise you if I tell you that 3 men appeared out of their little den where they had been playing Tavli, (Backgammon), and all rushed toward the Mercedes! Two of the men made it and the third reluctantly came to me. I wound down my window and asked for €20 worth and handed him the note. Meanwhile next to me, one man was busily washing the Mercedes windscreen giving extra attention to the dollop of bird shit, whilst the other stood at the driver's window awaiting instruction. The tinted electric window silently glided down allowing me to see the driver who looked barely old enough to drive, stick his hand out and hand the man a €5 note and quickly shut the window! €5? You would think that a man who can afford a €25,000 car can afford to buy more petrol than it takes to start it! Daddies car!

On another occasion I was at my local 'Pit Stop' for a set of new tyres. The M.O.T. guy had passed my car but made me promise to replace the tyres and go back and show him that same day. I was instructed to drive my Mazda onto the hydraulic jack/lift. I got out the car and Petros asks me; "You want the Alpha lastiga, the Beta lastiga or the ginesiga?" This mixture of English and Greek is called 'Gringlish'. He wanted to know if I wanted the 'A' class tyres i.e. 'Pirelli', 'Goodyear' etc. or the 'B' class tyres which were obscure names or the Chinese equivalents which are half the price, and there were re moulds. I wouldn't risk the re moulds and couldn't afford the 'Pirelli' so I went for the Chinese equivalents which are fine.

As we chatted a Mercedes came in. He wanted two front tyres. He was asked the same question as I was regarding the quality of tyre he wanted. He was given the prices of each class of tyre. He wanted to have the Dunlop but wasn't prepared to pay THAT price for them so he started to negotiate the price. Petros was not prepared to give him Dunlop tyres at Chinese prices, and I don't blame him, but Mr. Mercedes was not having it.
"MA BOSON GERTHOS THELETE?" (How much profit do you want?). He then wanted more information on the Chinese equivalents.
"INE GALA?" (Are they good?) He asks.
"NE BOLA GALA" (Yes very good) answers Petros.
"E YIATI INE BIO FTINA GALO" (Why are they cheaper then?).
Poor Petros tried to give him many reasons….the labour costs in China are cheaper, also with brands like Dunlop and Pirelli you are paying for the name. He likened it to buying Coca Cola or 'Stelios Supermarket' own brand, they both look and taste the same but Stelios is cheaper, blah, blah, blah. My four tyres had been fitted but they were STILL arguing the price. In the end he fitted re moulds!! Honestly, re moulds on a high performance car costing €25/30,000. I've got a Mercedes my Arse!!!

Our third popular vehicle here in Cyprus is the 'Four wheel drive' or 'S.U.V.'

The BMW seems to be a popular one over here. This is for the driver that has a bit of an identity crisis. He doesn't know if he wants a double cab or a family saloon. This vehicle is both. It's classier than a pick up and a Mercedes, (in their opinion), and as robust as a pick up. Another plus for the Cypriot is that its four wheel drive lends itself to off roading, and as Cypriots drive off road a lot....up pavements, up central reservations, up mountains, up trees, are you with me here?

They can be driven up the steep twisty roads of the Troodos mountains without the engine screaming and having to change gear every hundred meters as I do in my Mazda. There is enough room so they can get all their six kids into it and all the shopping, but the best bit is they can puff their chests out and say:
"EXO BMW!" (I have a BMW!). It's every bit as good as saying:
"EXO MESENDARA!"

Another plus point is that they sit higher than everybody else, unless you're a lorry driver or pickup driver, but they don't count. You can sit higher than a Mercedes driver which gives you that air of superiority, even though your debt is probably higher too, and even that fact I have seen used as a 'boasting' tool when in discussion at the Cafene!

So far it sounds like everybody drives around in €25,000 cars and trucks. A lot do because the Banks make it so easy, well they did but not so much now. Anyway, there are the odd sensible ones who wouldn't get into such debt, which brings us to category four;

'The 'Old banger'

It is not unusual to see people driving a 25/30 and sometimes 50 year old vehicle...seriously! It is not because of their antique worth but simply because they can't afford to replace it. How they get through their M.O.T.'s I don't know...well yes I do actually, nepotism goes a long way here in Cyprus, enough said. Rust isn't a big problem here for obvious reasons, it's not entirely nonexistent just minimal. There is a guy in my village that is driving around in a 27 year old Nissan Micra. It used to be Red but the Sun has bleached the paintwork so badly it is now Pink! The front bumper is missing and the rear one is tied on with string. The headlights don't work nor do the indicators, but hey nobody uses indicators over here! He can't afford a new car or even a second hand one and the council wanted paying to take it away. It has no scrap value, but you know what....he loves it!

Then there are the young lads that buy an old car for a few hundred Euros and then think nothing of spending their entire months' salary and more on customizing it. They spend thousands on 'Go faster stripes' and 'Alloy wheels', 'Aerofoil's' that wouldn't look out of place on a rocket! I have seen little Blue lights on the underside of the car? Is this so you can see the oil leaks?

Then there is 'Mr. Sensible', (that's me ☺). According to the 'Cyprus Statistical Service', there is a 30% rise in 'sensible' car sales this year, even in this time of crisis. Sensible means cars such as the Mazda Demio, Suzuki Swift etc.

There is one resounding common factor that connects all of the driver/categories we have discussed and that is...
"THEY ARE ALL SHIT DRIVERS!"
And that my friends is continued in another book. ☺

^===^===^

Jini (Hunting)

Second only to the 'Body Building Brigade', Jini is the most
macho thing a man can do in Cyprus….apparently. I must
be a sissy because I do neither! Body building is a no no
since my heart stopped me lifting even a cup of tea, and to
kill animals for sport is just not my thing. I know it's not
my thing because I have tried it….twice! Why it's deemed
macho to walk around fields and valleys shooting at
defenseless birds and rabbits is beyond me. Maybe it's
because they get to hold a GUN!? I will share with you my
two Jini experiences and I think you will agree that I am
right to leave it to the macho men.

Whilst having a cup of coffee with my neighbor Philipos, he said, "ELA NA BAME JINI AVRIO" (Come hunting tomorrow). I explained that I had never been before and besides I didn't own a gun. "THEN BIRAZI EXO THIO EGO" (Doesn't matter I have two), he exclaimed. He was most insistent and badgered me until I accepted his invitation. This is when I was to discover that there were two 3 o'clocks in a day! I was instructed to come to his house at this unearthly hour in the morning. He told me we would be driving up into the mountains where he knew of some great hunting grounds and that nobody else knew about them.

Three in the morning and I gently tapped on Philipos door so as not to wake the whole household. Philipos slowly opened the door and he was in full battle dress! That is to say, starting from his head to his toes; On his head was one of those stupid looking hats with the floppy bits coming down over his ears, I think they are called 'Deerstalkers', but under that he wore a Green Balaclava! He wore a three quarter length jacket with a special belt for hanging your dead animals on, and on top of that, a waistcoat that had hundreds of little pockets for putting your cartridges in. Then there were those baggy trousers, 'Combats' I believe, and all finished off with a pair of fur lined willies! ALL this attire was in the customary camouflage colors of Green and Brown. I would have to keep a very close eye on him or he would just become invisible amongst all the foliage. Me? Well I was wearing my Levi Jeans and a light Grey jumper! He insisted that I wear one of his jackets because I would frighten off all the wildlife...seriously? He gave me a crash course on how to open, load and close the gun and we jumped into the pickup and set off for the mountains and the secret hunting grounds.

We had been driving for about 30mins. Which equates to a fair distance in Cyprus considering you could drive from one end of the Island to the other in about 4 hours. Suddenly, Philipos made a sharp turn Left taking us off the main road and onto a dusty track. We drove a further 5mins through Woods and Vales and there in the middle of nowhere was a building…..it was a Taverna!

"BROYEVMA" (Breakfast), he said.

WHAT! at this hour? I rarely eat breakfast, well maybe a couple of slices of toast about 10am when I'm fully awake, but at 4am? Philipos explained that it was a traditional thing to do, it was part of the 'Hunting trip experience'. We parked and went into the Taverna. I couldn't help but point out that it was surprisingly busy considering nobody knew the place we were going to.

"THEN EFTASAME AGOMA!" (We haven't got there yet!) , he retorted.

I asked him where the menu was, which sent him into fits of laughter.

"No menu", he answered, beaming from ear to ear because he had answered in English.

I looked around me at the surrounding tables and noticed they were all eating the same thing…SOUP!

"Soup for breakfast?" I said.

"NE, SOUPA TRAXANA! IS GOOD FOR YOU ENE KIP YOU HOT!"

I think he meant it warms you up. Anyway, 'TRAXANA' is made with Wheat and Yoghurt. It is mixed together and then rolled out into strands and then put out into the Sun where it is left to dry until it is rock hard. When you want to make TRAXANA, you add water and boil it and voila soup! Sometimes they cut up little cubes of Halloumi cheese and drop it into the mix like you would croutons.

Now, I am ok with Wheat and I love Halloumi, but if there is anything that turns my stomach it's Yoghurt! Put all these ingredients together and you have, in my opinion, a plate full of baby PUKE! No really, it looks like puke and it smells like puke and it tastes like two day old puke! I would rather bang a blunt rusty nail into the end of my knob than eat it! ....Sorry, I had to make my point ☺ I explained that I wasn't hungry and that I was going outside for a fag, I smoked then.

Philipos eventually finished his pu … sorry breakfast, and came out so we could continue our journey. We drove for a further 30mins but we were going upwards now over some very rough terrain. There were lots of mountains, well little hills. The pickup was almost at 90 degrees it was so steep, then suddenly it leveled out and we were on top of the hill on a plateau which is where Philipos parked. I have to admit that it was stunning up there. The scenery was amazing. I wished that I had a camera and not a gun. I looked around and realized that there were four other pickup trucks there! I quickly pointed this out.
'THEN BIRAZI' (Doesn't matter), said Philipos. So much for his 'secret' place!

Philipos handed me a side by side double barreled shotgun and six cartridges. He instructed me to keep the gun loaded but open whilst we walked.
'ELA BERBATOUME' (Come let's walk).

I dutifully followed Philipos. Now, considering this was a secret place, the wide dusty track we were following looked like the Chinese Army had marched through on one of their field exercises! It was trodden flat and clear of all undergrowth.

Suddenly, Philipos turned to face me with his finger to his lips gesturing for me to be quiet, he had seen something! He slowly lay down flat onto his stomach and had me follow suit. I lay by his side. He then slowly crawled up the track Commando style, so I followed his lead. He stopped and did that gesture they do in war films and pointed directly in front of us. I looked and yes indeed I saw in the distance a pair of Rabbit ears twitching like they do. It was sat in the middle of the track and was a sitting Duck....well Rabbit. I watched as Philipos took careful aim and BANG he fired. The dust settled and the Rabbit was still there!
'GAMMO TA!!' (Fuck it!) said Philipos irritated as he fired his second cartridge. I couldn't believe it the Rabbit was STILL there! Philipos bashed me on the back.
'BEXE TON GAMMO SHISTI!' (Shoot the f***ing ***t).
I took aim as if I had done this a hundred times before and pulled the trigger but....being a novice at this, I had pulled the trigger all the way back instead of one click! This resulted in both cartridges firing at once! Not only that, but as I didn't have the butt of the gun pressed tightly against my shoulder as instructed, the gun shot backwards and landed on my back. Philipos just looked at me in disbelief and disgust at my pitiful efforts. We got to our feet and would you believe it, the Rabbit was still there! We walked toward the invincible one and as we got closer I started to laugh. We had been shooting at two long blades of wild grass that had grown in the middle of the track having survived the Chinese army and now us. Should have gone to Specsavers!

After some aimless wandering about without seeing a living thing, we were heading back to the truck. There on the Plateau were at least six other men smoking, drinking Tzivania and chatting. I looked around again at the beautiful location. Opposite us was another hill and on that plateau there were a few men milling about. Separating us was a deep valley. As we all stood around exchanging stories about the ones that got away, a huge flock of birds were spotted and they were flying towards us. You have never seen so many men load their weapons so quickly. The guys on the other side of the valley had spotted them too. The birds got closer and closer swooping down into the valley between the hills. All the shotgun barrels went up at once like some sort of synchronized event, and the firing began with a vengeance, they needed a kill!! I stood back and two things crossed my mind. If by some slim chance any of these crazed so called marksmen should actually hit anything, it would just drop deep down into the valley where they had next to zero chance of retrieving it! The second and most scary thought was that there were two sets of trigger happy men on either side of a valley firing guns across it in each other's direction! Many deaths are recorded during hunting season and I didn't want to be a statistic so I went and sat in the pickup. 'Health and Safety' what's that?

My second experience of Jini just a few weeks later wasn't nearly as eventful, but nonetheless it was the deciding factor that hunting was not for me.

Again, over a cup of Cypriot coffee with another neighbor, Georgios, having heard that our mutual neighbor Philipos had taken me hunting, decided that he was not to be outdone and that he was going to take this 'Charlie', that's me, hunting also. I protested the fact that I hadn't enjoyed my first outing but Georgios was insistent. The thing that tipped the scales was the fact that we wouldn't be going miles away. The hunting grounds were quite local just about five miles away. Also we wouldn't be leaving at 3am in the morning but at 5pm in the evening. It wasn't going to be so much a hunting trip but a life's lesson for his two little boys one was 11 years old and the other just 9 years old! They start them young over here.

So that evening we all piled into Georgios pickup and set off for 'TROULI'. We drove for about five minutes up the 'B' road that joined us to the neighboring village and then turned off into some fields and the wilderness. Georgios parked in an Olive grove and opposite the grove grew some very tall Bamboos. This is where we were going to loiter as apparently a certain type of bird nests in the Bamboo.

Georgios took his super duper €2000 up and under double barreled shotgun out of its case. It was gleaming and it was his 'Baby', nobody but nobody was allowed to touch it! Banikos, the eldest son, had a high powered air rifle with telescopic sights, he was ordered to share it with me. The youngest son, Matheos, had the job of picking up the mass of birds we were going to massacre. His other job was to go into the Bamboo growth and disturb it so the birds would fly out and to their deaths!

We stood at the edge of the Bamboo growth as Matheos disappeared into it. After just a few minutes the birds came charging out....all ONE of them! I'm sure it waved as it flew past us. Georgios fired at it twice and missed followed by Banikos who also missed.

Banikos handed me the air rifle, it was my turn to have a go at the next opportune moment. We stood around rolling fags and chatting for what seemed like hours and there was not a bird in sight. I was enjoying the tranquility of the country side when suddenly a bird came into sight heading directly for us.

'GRIGORA BEXE TO!' (Quickly shoot it!).

I looked down the telescopic sight and took careful aim just in front of it as I was instructed. I fired! With a swerve and a fluttering of wings the bird plummeted earthwards and came crashing down about a hundred yards ahead of us. Two emotions went through my mind at that moment;

"Wow I hit it!" and "Oh no, I hit it!"

The two boys went running toward it so I joined them. I looked down at the most beautiful bird I had ever seen close up, it was a 'Kingfisher' I was told. The poor thing was writhing and fluttering in agony! I was overcome with sadness, what had I done?

'EN SONTANO AGOMA' (It's still alive), exclaimed Georgios.

No shit Sherlock! I thought, almost in tears. I gave the gun to Banikos and got down on my knees next to the poor bird. I don't know what I expected to do because this bird was way past mouth to mouth and before I could do anything 'SMASH' Banikos had brought the butt of the gun crashing down on the defenseless birds head! That was it, no more bird and no more hunting for me!

Iyia ke Usfalia (Health and Safety)

Now here is a subject! Let me explain MY experiences concerning Health and Safety by telling you about my two year stint working for a building company before my health put paid to it.

The working day started at 7am and ended at 3pm. We were PAID from 7am so this is when the boss expected us to be on site. This meant we would have to leave the company yard at 6am to get to Nicosia, the capitol where most of our work was for 7am. I need at least an hour in the mornings to be functional before going to work so I was up at 5am! By the time I had got to work I felt that I had already done a day! Hey ho never mind jobs are hard to come by.

So my first day and all twenty employees meet at the yard at 6am. From here we are split into groups to go to various jobs. We then pile into the pickups and set off for Nicosia. At least the pickups were supplied by the company even if they had seen better days. I am now squeezed into a five seater pickup with eight men who to be polite, were over sized, plus their kit bags that contained their lunches and hey what lunches! Anyone would think we were going away on a weeklong expedition! They also all have a 5liter container of water, very necessary when in the Cyprus Sun. So conditions were cramped to say the least. We hadn't been driving for five minutes when the driver pulled into a lay by and a 'BERIPTERO' (a convenience kiosk). Everybody fell out of the pickup to buy their 'POGA' (Poker iced coffee in a tin), 'KOUBES' (Bulgur wheat rolled around minced meat), hundreds of fags and Snickers bars, all for the journey then squeezed back into the pickup and onwards.

We eventually arrive at the job which was a detached three story house. The mission is to hack off all the external cement render which was well past its sell by date, and re render with a decorative render called 'Grafiato'. First job was to erect scaffolding around the building. They decided that to save on scaffolding they would only erect it on one face of the building and move it around as each face is completed. Four of us were tasked with the job of unloading the scaffold and tools whilst the other four got on with the job of erecting the scaffold. This was my first taste of the complete disregard of the words 'Health and Safety'! Words that are completely alien to the Cypriot workman, well most of them. However, I must add that the government ARE tightening up on Health and Safety but then again Cypriots are the hardest people in the World to tell what to do.

Eventually the scaffold went up and we clambered up it to begin the task of hacking off render. The first thing I noticed was that nobody was wearing a hard hat, but some WERE wearing shorts and flip flops! This caused me some concern, if you can imagine three floors of scaffolding with men standing on each level bashing great big lumps of concrete off the wall and no regard for the men beneath them! It was ok if you were on the top level but those on the second and third levels were being narrowly missed by falling debris! No hard hats, no goggles and no safety shoes equals disaster! It was only going to be a matter of time before somebody would be visiting Nicosia General. Being the new boy I didn't want to rock the boat and perhaps lose my job on the first day, a job I had been lucky enough to secure in the first place, but I had to do something even for my own safety, but what? Then it came to me…. I hacked off quite a large piece of concrete and bashed it down hard on the metal platform of the scaffold which made quite a noise, and at the same time I let out a scream that would have turned your milk into Greek yoghurt at a 100mtres! Everybody stopped bashing at once, there was complete silence. The guy a few away from me looked at me and said;

"ISE ENTAXI FILOUI MOU?" (Are you ok my little friend?)

To this day I don't know why he said 'little friend' because he was at least a foot shorter than me!

"NE NE" (Yes yes), I assured him pointing at my feet.

At our morning tea break I dared make a suggestion. I suggested we all go to the top level hack off the render then all move down one and so on. I was sure that with some order/discipline we would finish quicker and most of all safer. They all looked at me in silence, then one shouts out;

"BRAVO RE ENGLESO!" (Bravo you English)

"MA ETSI GAMNETE STIN ANGLIA?" (Is that what you do in England?).

Yes I explained and avoided getting into the hard hats, goggles and safety shoes because I would end up with a riot on my hands. So if that's how it is done in the UK, it was good enough for them. They had a strange respect for the UK....well mostly.

So we have eight men standing at the top of the scaffolding all banging on the wall in front of us and all in unison, it was almost musical. As I brought my club hammer back ready to strike another blow I was sure the wall moved away from me causing me to miss the bolster I was holding in the other hand. I tried again but the wall moved again....wait a minute! It was the scaffolding that was moving AWAY from the wall! I stopped instantly and watched as the scaffold rocked back and forth with every blow of the hammers, can I say I actually FARTED in fear! Had the guys not tied in the scaffold? Had they fuck! I asked one of the culprits;

"YIATI? AFOUS THA TO TARAXOME AGOMA LIO" (Why? we are going to move it again in a bit).

It's not that they are stupid, but they think they are immortal, invincible! Ok, maybe a little stupid!

Staying on the health and safety subject, there follows a few more events and observations to prove my point.

You may have heard or read about this incident as it was a gross disregard for health and safety and a perfect example of the attitude that exists which cost lives and injuries. Not funny I know but relevant.

There is a place in Limasol, a district in Cyprus called 'MARI'. Situated in Mari is a naval base. In this base were stored 98 shipping containers that were full to the brim with artillery shells of varying sizes. Not to get too deep into the politics and whys and wherefores, the USA had seized this shipment of ammunitions and asked Cyprus to store it temporarily. This happened in 2009. Im 2011 there was a massive explosion! This was heard all over Cyprus. ALL 98 containers disintegrated killing 13 and injuring 62! It did untold damage to surrounding buildings including the nearby power station causing blackouts for miles, Why?....

If you have ever visited Cyprus in the height of Summer you will know that the temperatures soar into the 40's Centigrade. If you should feel so inclined, you could fry an egg on the bonnet of your car. The 98 containers were sat in the middle of an open field completely exposed to the elements, no shade of any kind in the searing heat for 2½ years! Something had to give...and it did. Health and Safety my Cypriot arse!

Another incident that comes to mind is when I visited my car mechanic for an oil change.

I entered his workshop and was astounded by the sight that befell me! There was Pavlos lying under a car! Yes I know that's what mechanics do but not like this! His hydraulic jack/lift was out of order so he had the car at a 45° angle wedged up by two 4" x 4" lumps of wood! The picture below is not the actual picture, but just to demonstrate what I mean.

(Thank you Google)

What I never did find out was HOW did he lift it to position the wood? One little slip and Pavlos would be HOUMOUS!

This complete disregard for health and safety is at epidemic levels here in Cyprus.

You see mums in their cars with their very young children standing on the front seat next to her and clinging onto the dashboard for dear life! Whilst driving she is on her mobile phone and smoking all at the same time!

There is the 80 year old man on his moped. No helmet and wearing short sleeves and flip flops and full shopping bags hanging off each end of the handle bar and weaving in and out of the traffic as if they shouldn't be there!

You could write a whole book on the Health and Safety issue in Cyprus….but I won't!

^===^===^

Thimarxio/Givernisi - Ibalili
(Council/Government employees)

Well every country has these, indeed dear reader you might be one and nothing wrong with that….unless you are in Cyprus!

Here in Cyprus unless you are related to the President himself or you know someone who knows someone that is, you have as much chance of getting a job with the Council or Government as the Pope has marrying a man! (at the moment anyway). Yes, nepotism is rife here in Cyprus. If your great great grandfather was employed by the Council when he retired the job went down to your great grandfather and he to your father and should you want to be a dustman, he will hand it down to you. A job with the Council is deemed a job for life and it usually pays better too. You would have to do something very bad to be sacked from a Council job and even then you are so protected that they would find some amazing mitigating circumstances for you so that you could keep your job.

Let's have a look at the Postal service. I know other countries have 'hiccups' with this service, even the UK, but in Cyprus it's more a case of not 'hiccups' but chronic 'f**k ups'! I am sure you have heard the term 'Snail mail', I mean, is there anything slower than a Snail? Well I didn't think there was but as I'm writing this it is the 2nd March 2016 and this morning I received not one but two Christmas cards! I wasn't sure if they were for last year or maybe this year!

This is how our system works. It's probably much the same the World over but I'm writing about Cyprus and what I know for sure. There is a main Post office where all the post for Cyprus is delivered and then distributed throughout Cyprus. I believe this to be in the Capitol Nicosia. So, from Nicosia it is delivered to all the main districts, i.e. Larnaca, Limasol, Paphos, Famagusta etc. Then from these main districts it is delivered to all the small Towns and villages within those districts. I am in a village called Livadia and believe it or not, our post office is a Yellow shed in the Post man's front garden! Please see proof below, although it had been painted Grey when I went to photograph it.

In this Post office (shed), our local Post man sorts the mail into the relevant roads/streets. If you ever want to know where anybody lives, make sure you give the postie a bottle of Othello at Xmas time. He knows everybody in his village, all 7,206 of them!

He delivers his mail on his Moped. Obviously he doesn't deliver all the mail for Livadia in one day because he wouldn't get it all in the silly little basket on the front of his moped, much like the one you had on your Tricycle when you were a kid! So he is back and forth filling his basket each time.

Something that really grates me is that when he delivers your Telephone or Electricity bill, on opening it, where it states 'TO BE PAID BY' it has got yesterdays date! Nobody likes receiving bills but they have probably been sitting in his shed for weeks while he earns an extra euro or two delivering junk mail for the local businesses telling you that you can get two packets of Pampers for the price of one!

The Refuse collectors.
I can only compare the dustmen here in Cyprus with the ones in the UK as I have experienced them both and they are not dissimilar.

Our dustmen visit twice a week. They come at an unearthly hour 3/4am and don't you know it! Cypriots/Greeks are known for their loud voices when they converse, you would be forgiven if you think that the two people talking to each other are having an argument. The dust cart is loaded with five men! Two standing on the foot boards at the back of the truck and three sitting in the cab. One is obviously driving and for the life of me I don't know what the other two do. The two hanging off the back are 'talking' to the ones in the cab, they are so loud so as to be heard over the noise of the dust cart engine it's mind blowing! You can hear them coming from three streets away, more so where I live in a cul de sac in quiet rural surroundings.

At the front of our houses they build into the front boundary wall a bin store/cupboard. It's quite decorative made of White aluminum with double doors. (See photo).

My bin store.

Here is where we put our full bin bags ready for collection. Now I don't know if it's a game they play, but the driver drives very slowly down the street, the two men on the back jump off while the truck is moving and each man takes a side of the road opening the bin store, taking out the bags and tossing them into the back of the truck and this all happens while the truck is still creeping up the road, he will NOT stop. It's funny to watch because sometimes, if there is more than one bag in a bin store the unfortunate bin man takes a little longer so you see him running back to the next house in a vain attempt to keep up with the truck. Sometimes the truck just gets too far ahead of the two bin men and it's just like watching two Clowns at the Big Top! Occasionally they will attempt to throw the bags from a distance to save time but miss the truck and spilling all sorts of disgusting rubbish on the road! How do I know all this? Why am I up at 3/4am watching the bin men? Well......

On three separate occasions, the bin men in their rush to open the bin store they have yanked/snapped off the handle on the doors and then just leaving it on the floor. They never shut the doors anyway, but now I can't stop the doors flapping in the wind and banging against the wall. After the THIRD repair I decided I would have to have a word in their dust like ears! It hasn't happened since but they still refuse to shut the doors, it would take to long!

When Christmas comes round you get the customary 'Merry Xmas from your dustmen' card hoping they might get a monetary gift for all their hard work....maybe I should give them one and MAYBE they will shut my f***ing doors!

The Highways and Byways men another special breed. Scenes like the photo below can be seen Worldwide and Cyprus is no exception.

How many are actually working?

These poor guys are on the road, (pun intended), very early in the morning, again due to the heat and having to achieve their project before the midday Sun strikes, and they normally do. Another neighbor of mine works for the Council and when he kisses his wife goodbye in the morning, before the damp patch on her cheek is dry he is home again! It's true! I see his car leave at 6.30am and he is back home by noon. (I sound like a curtain twitcher!)

This doesn't stop him from booking a full day's work, I know because he told me. They are given a mission/project in the morning at the yard whilst they are drinking their 'POGA', i.e. "Fill in the hole in Llidl's car park with Tarmac then you can go home". So they do in record time, all six of them to lay a square meter of Tarmac and go home.

A job on the Council is like winning the Lottery, not just for the reasons mentioned, I'm sure they work sometimes, but all the bonus's/benefits and perks that come with the job. A Council worker is allowed to go to a private Doctor in the event that he should need one and then claim a percentage of the cost back from the Council. They get three weeks paid holiday a year, and they get what they call a '13th' salary, this is an extra months pay at the end of the year which is very handy at Xmas time for that extra lump of Halloumi. Another perk is a list of places that you can visit for a holiday approved by the Council. If you go to one of these places and stay in one of the approved Hotels you can stay at a discounted price....why? Beats me?

^===^===^

To Kafenio (The coffee shop)

You will find a Kafenio in every village and Town but the real traditional ones are in the small villages. It is an 'adventure playground' for mainly old men.

The Kafenio is of course the 'coffee shop'. Even in these days of 'Starbucks' and 'Costa Coffee' where you have the privilege of paying ridiculous amounts of money for your coffee, the traditional Kafenio survives. Here you can still get a traditional 'Cyprus coffee' for 50 cents. Note I said 'Cyprus' coffee, and if I were in Greece I would have said 'Greek' coffee, but in actual fact the Turks invented this method of drinking coffee as far back as 1640 when the first coffee shop opened in Istanbul. The reason you ask for a Cyprus coffee is a political one and it came about in 1974 after the Turks invaded Cyprus. As a stand against the Turks we Cypriots didn't fire guns and drop bombs on them, no, we REALLY stuck it to them and merely dropped the 'Turkish' from 'Turkish Coffee', that'll show them! If you went into a small village Kafenio and asked for a Turkish coffee, which it is, the whole room would become silent! The clicking of the Tavli boards (Backgammon), would stop, the irate loud voices arguing about last night's football match would stop, in fact all movement would cease like it does in films sometimes and all eyes would be on you! This set of circumstances would remain so until you either apologize and correct your mistake, or someone takes pity on you and corrects you. If you haven't shit your pants and STILL want a coffee, you will be bought one sat down and educated!

The Kafenio is the hub and most important place in the village. Here is where all the Worlds problems are solved by ageing wise men who just happen to know everything! It is the centre of the Universe. When you become a certain age and you longer work and you have got out of bed before that f***king annoying Cockerel and you have fed your Chickens, you hobble down to the village square and to the Kafenio for your morning coffee. This is where ALL the village elders gather and if one should be a bit later than usual, it causes a buzz around the room and everybody is wondering if poor Dimitri didn't make it through the night! The 'Kafeji' (The owner), is busy making coffee of various tastes, 'SKETO' (No sugar), 'MEDRIO' (A little sugar) and 'GLIGI' (Sweet). They all take their usual tables/seats after they have produced the Tavli boards, Playing cards, the Chess boards and battle commences whilst discussing the latest scandal or event. It's very rare to see a 'young' man or a woman in the Kafenio they have better things to do. It's very much a Social club for ageing men. Personally I am yet to be drawn into this 'happening'….yet! On occasion I have been into our local Kafenio just out of curiosity and of course research for what I am writing here for you. Everybody knows everybody else and when there is a new member of the community he usually becomes the topic of conversation, all offering their opinions on who you are and where you are from, if you are rich or poor, married or single. I personally underwent serious interrogation when I first went into the Kafenio, and strangely enough, at least three old men knew my family from way back when.

I sat and watched an intense game of Tavli. It was between the champ Alecos who wore a very strange and shabby straw hat and was at least a 100 years old, and a guy called Zakkos.

I sipped my coffee and my eyes scanned the room and there sitting in the corner, alone, was another old guy who was at least 200 years old! Obviously I exaggerate, but he did look very old with his big White beard and White hair that was in a ponytail, and a leathery face. He was playing 'Solo', I asked one of the Tavli spectators who he was.

"EN O MARIOS, ANI TIXES" (That's Marios he is a fortune teller.)

I was informed that if you bought Marios a coffee he would read your coffee grounds.

Just to enlighten you, Cyprus coffee is cooked/boiled and when it is poured the coffee forms a sort of sludge at the bottom of the cup, (DO NOT DRINK THIS!). The idea is when you finish your coffee you upturn your cup onto the saucer and let it stand for a few minutes. The sludge runs down the inside of the cup forming shapes and these shapes are read by the fortune teller. So coffee finished I turned my cup upside down into the saucer and wondered over and sat opposite him.

"BIOS ISE?" (Who are you?), he asked.

"You tell me you're the fortune teller", I replied laughing....he was not amused! He glared at me with his dark and bloodshot eyes almost suffocating me with his intense stare.

"ISE TELIA GAROS!", (You're a complete Donkey!), he said.

I agreed with him as he picked up my cup. He studied my cup carefully letting out the odd grunt and eventually he talked to me.

"ISE ENGLESOGIBREOS", (You are an English Cypriot) he said, as if he had told me something I didn't know. Just the way I speak Greek gives me away.

"THA BAIS TAXITHI" (You will go on a trip), again, something that was odds on in his favour. He went on to tell me a few things that anybody could have had a stab at and been more or less correct. I just took it for what it was, a bit of fun, and an old man trying to make ends meet. I put the price of a coffee on the table in front of him and stood up to leave.

"ENA LEPTO THEN TELIOSA" (Hang on I haven't finished).

I sat back down.

"THORO BROVLIMATA" (I see problems).

"What sort of problems?" I asked.

"SIOBI!" (Shut up!).

He turned the cup silently staring intently at the sludge shapes within the cup. He pointed out a smudge of sludge and said in an urgent voice...

"ETHO! ETHO!" (Here!, here!).

I looked at what looked like a smudge of coffee grounds keeping an open mind and that's when I saw it! A smudge of coffee grounds!

I thanked him again, ordered him a coffee and went back to the Tavli game. Alecos with his straw hat was now playing somebody else having thrashed Zakkos. Alecos made light work of dismissing this opponent also and was rewarded with screams of elation from the spectators. Screams louder than if Cyprus had won the World cup!

"EBOMENOS!" (Next), shouted Alecos.

Someone slapped me on the back and said, "BEXE ESI" (You play).

I tried to explain that I wasn't very good at Tavli, but they all insisted. I took position in front of Alecos. We were to play the best of five games.

"GALES EBITIXIES" (Good luck), said the sporting Alecos. Alecos won the first game and then the second game, then mother luck shone down on me and I won games three and four. So it was all down to the last game, a one game shootout! The previously loud and boisterous spectators had become eerily quiet, you could hear a pin drop....should you drop one. It was a very close game and I WON! I jumped up and down waving my arms around and expecting everybody to join me, or perhaps hoist me up onto their shoulders and do a lap of honor....nothing! Absolutely nothing! They all looked at Alecos who's head was bowed down low, then they looked at me as if I was smothered in shit, then back at Alecos.

Alecos slowly removed his hat revealing his bald head. He reached over and placed the hat on my head. Everybody went as far away from me as possible totally blanking me. One man condescended to talk to me. He told me that Alecos NEVER lost, and winked as he said it. He had vowed that if anybody should beat him he would give them his very old friend, his hat! Because nobody wanted to deprive Alecos of his hat anyone that played him made SURE they lost so as not to upset Alecos, it was just a Kafenio custom......how was I to know? I was advised that if I wanted to do the right thing I would return tomorrow and challenge Alecos to a rematch, and LOSE! As I didn't fancy the idea of being alienated in the village and being sold bad cuts of meat by the Butcher and Bread complete with Mouse droppings from the Baker, I did as I was told.

Looks like Marios the fortune teller was right!

^===^===^

To Gourio (The Barber shop).

Where there is a Kafenio in the village, not too far away is the Barber shop. As an aside, if you are ever in Cyprus, and you want the best shave ever try an old fashioned village Barber shop. If you are a Woman dear reader….you needn't ☺.

You would be forgiven for thinking that you have mistakenly walked into a Kafenio. This is yet another place where all the old retired men hang out and drink coffee whilst listening to the latest gossip from the Barber. What better place to hear the newest juicy gossip than the Barbers? After all, he cuts most of the villagers hair, and as they cut they interrogate, sorry, ask questions, much like a women's hairdressers.

I must add that this behavior applies mainly to the 'village' Barber shops. The bigger Town Barbers have a more modern and conservative outlook on life and also their prices. You can still get a haircut for €3.50 in a village.

When you enter the Barber shop you get a very friendly welcome and an offer of coffee. If you accept, Andreas will shout out across the village square at the Kafeji with your order and after a few minutes it will be delivered to you. (Andreas must have a tab). The point is, if you are in a rush, don't go for a haircut! But nobody ever seems to be in a rush, after all this IS Cyprus. Other than myself there are four men present in the shop. One sitting on the one and only Barber's chair and one twiddling his 'GOMBOLOI' (Worry beads) waiting for his turn. The other two men are just there for a natter, and Andreas can natter! He will just stop mid flow whilst cutting your hair so he could wave his arms about to get his point over on whatever the topic of discussion is at the time. He eventually finishes cutting the man's hair, (all three of them), and after asking him if he would like 'anything for the weekend', and it's only Monday, he sends him on his way. Do they still ask that in the UK? 'ANYTHING FOR THE WEEKEND SIR?' ...I remember the first time I was asked that and wondered what the fuck he was talking about!! It was ages before I found out he meant Condoms!

The next guy in line, Stelios, was there to have his hair dyed! Personally I prefer to grow old gracefully but Stelios thought otherwise. Andreas the Barber spoke to me;

"ENJE VIASESE ENE" (Your not in a hurry are you), more a statement than a question. I said no but even if I had said yes it was Stelios' turn so I could either come back another day or wait. I waited and I'm glad I did because it gave me the biggest laugh of the day! Stelios' hair was cut and washed and then Andreas, after putting on a pair of surgical gloves, started to massage something into Stelios' head/hair. Whatever it was I am sure I heard it sizzle! It turned into a Jet Black foam and then it was combed through his hair. It had to be left for about 15mins. Before he could continue so a good excuse for another coffee.

After 15mins. Of heated debate about the advantages and disadvantages of being a member of the EU, and what would happen if the Turks were allowed to join, Stelios' head was cooked and ready to proceed. I watched as Andreas washed out the Black gunk from Stelios' hair. He then combed and blow dried it….voila! Stelios was now….A LEGO MAN! Honestly, if you are familiar with the Lego figures you will know what I mean, if not and you really care Google it.

Yes his hair was definitely Jet Black which looked completely unnatural on a 65/70 year old, and to top it all, where the dye had been absorbed by the skin around his hair line and stained it, it looked like somebody had highlighted the hair line with a Black Magic Marker Pen!

He looked ridiculous but Stelios was more than happy, in fact he was so happy with his new youthful look he didn't wait for Andreas to ask the question, "Anything for the weekend?" Stelios asked Andreas! He obviously had plans, the mind boggles.

No, Silver Grey for me thanks!

^===^===^

Kibriagi ora (Cyprus time)

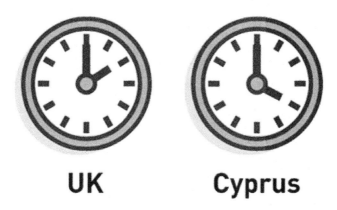

UK   Cyprus

Another concept that is alien to Cypriots...time! There is time and then there is Cyprus time. If you have lived or are in any way connected to Cyprus you will probably be aware of the often spoken phrase; "SIGA SIGA" (Slowly slowly). 'Why do today that which you can do tomorrow' seems to carry a lot of weight over here. You can replace 'WEIGHT' with 'WAIT' if you like...see what I did there? ☺ Cyprus is known for its much slower pace of life, that is why I moved here, but then there is 'laid back' and there is so laid back you are almost falling over! This applies very much when dealing with officialdom as I found out recently when I applied for my Pension.

I was advised by the Citizens Advice Bureau that I should apply for my Pension three months before my 65th birthday...Three months!!! Does it take that long in the UK? I think probably not, but it doesn't end there, oh no. I dutifully filled out the reams of paperwork and handed them in.

"TORA THA BERIMENIS" (Now you will wait), said the girl who was dressed for a night club visit. I thanked her and went away.

At the time of writing this draft it was 21st March 2016....and I'm still waiting! It has been eight months since I made my application! I applied three months before November 3rd 2015 my 65th birthday! I have visited the relevant offices several times and each time I have been fobbed off with "SIGA SIGA" or "VIASESE BOLA" (Your in too much of a hurry). If I get it before I publish this book I will add a note on the last page!

Some advice;
When engaging some ones services for any sort of work that involves them visiting your home and he says;

"THA ERTO TO MESIMERI" (I'll come in the afternoon), try and tie them to a more specific time. To me, afternoon is any time after noon and say up to 4/5 which is now becoming evening.

"THA ERTO BERIBOU TRIS I ORA" (I'll come about 3), but before thanking him and hanging up, be sure to ask him WHICH DAY!.....seriously. I waited until 3pm for the guy who was coming round to fix my washing machine, and he DID come on time....but the next day!!

Another good example is the Hospital. To see a GP you must go to a Hospital unless you are fortunate enough to be able to afford private health care. At the Hospital you can be seen by a GP at the minimal cost of €3. You can expect to be at the Hospital for about three hours! If you want to see a specialist, that is a Cardiologist or a Urologist etc. it is by appointment only. Well that must be good because if you have an appointment it's for a specific time so you know when you will be seen so you can turn up say half an hour before....not so!

I tell you this with hand on heart, I turned up for my 10am appointment with the Urologist and I was eventually seen at 2pm! What's the point of an appointment? When I dared question the delay, the reaction I got was;

"SIGA SIGA THEN ISE O MONOS AROSTOS!" (Slowly slowly you are not the only sick person).

Granted I'm not, but I'm the only one who had the Olives to complain! Cypriots seem immune to this kind of delay taking it all in their stride. I suppose as you acclimatize to the weather you also acclimatize to the 'time phenomenon'.

Why are you telling us this, it's not funny? I hear you ask, no it's not funny but I'm including this to demonstrate that time is a concept that is yet to be mastered here, plus I believe that SOME people laugh at others misfortunes!

Did you know that even SANTA is late in Cyprus? I am telling you the truth! Here in Cyprus it is the custom to get your Christmas gifts delivered on New Year's Day! Why?

Yes dear reader the very reason I came to Cyprus to live was for the slower pace of life, but it can also be the biggest pain in the arse! The only way 'Time flies' in Cyprus is if you took off your watch and threw it! Sometimes though, just sometimes, you wished time would fly.

^===^===^

Thrisgia (Religion)

My father always warned me not to get drawn into discussions involving Football, Politics and Religion, but this is not a discussion, it is me giving you an insight into Cyprus attitude and my observations on this subject....religion. I have said before in book one, I am not particularly religious but I do have a respect for it even though it sometimes confuses me because of the hypocrisy it sometimes portrays. I'll try and explain myself with a particular incident. Granted it was while I lived in the UK, but it demonstrates the misleading logic and hypocrisy of the Cypriot attitude to religion.

Where I lived in Hastings East Sussex there was a thriving Cypriot community which was growing by the year. (Family planning, another alien concept!). As Cypriots we didn't have an actual Greek Orthodox church nearby that we could use should we choose to. One day at a community meeting it was announced that an old abandoned church in our Town had come up for sale. Now SOME would have you believe that this was some kind of divine intervention at our hour of need sort of thing! The fact that the church was in such disrepair and crumbling and was getting to expensive to maintain and thus on the market, didn't even come up for discussion. The church was made available to us by the great almighty. It was voted on and we all agreed to purchase it. That's what we do, we all chip in for the community and with a little help from the Greek Bank Manager the church was purchased.

To cut a long story short, which is a stupid thing to do when writing a book, but I want to get to the point I'm trying to make and that is the hypocrisy. So long story short…..eventually the church was repaired to a useable standard. We invited the Greek Archbishop to bless it, and at great expense to the Cypriot community, a priest and his family were brought from Greece. They were housed and a wage negotiated so now we have a fully functioning church complete with priest. We had a grand opening and the whole of the Cypriot community were present for the first sermon all giving support. It was one of my rare visits to church that didn't involve a wedding, funeral or christening.

I listened intently to the mornings sermon whose subject matter was on the 'demon drink' and all the bad things that come with it. It was a nice sermon but a pointless one in my opinion to a congregation of people that I know their goal and ambition is to see if they could drink KEO's stock pile dry. Keo is a Cypriot brewery. But that's not the hypocrisy….

A few months had passed and a new shop had opened in Town, and' Off License' to be exact. As it was rumored amongst the Cypriot community that it stocked imported Cypriot alcohol such as Keo Brandy and Tzivania, I decided I would pay it a visit.

I entered the shop and my eyes flitted from right to left as I caught sight of all manner of Cypriot goods such as, Olives, Halloumi and Cypriot bread. "The Cyps are going to love this!" I thought to myself. At the far end of the shop, framed by shelf upon shelf of alcohol stood the owner.

As I approached the counter I did a double take! Standing there behind the counter was the same man that not long ago was preaching to us about the pitfalls of the 'Demon drink'.....it was our priest!

You could have knocked me down with a feather...or Olive branch!

TELOS (END).

I hope you enjoyed my efforts as much as I did writing them. If you did, or even if you didn't, could I politely ask you to leave a review? We independents rely on reviews to get our names out there and it would be greatly appreciated.

If you get a minute please visit my website to see what other works I offer. Thank you and thanks for your support.

www.chrischristodouloumybooks.com.cy

Printed in Great Britain
by Amazon

28863996R00030